Jay's Administration Presents

What Happens When Your Loved One Dies

A Novel By:

Jerome Staten

What Happens When Your Loved One Dies

Published by Jay's Administration

Cover Design by Jerome Staten

jerome_staten@yahoo.com

www.facebook.com/jeromestaten

What Happens When Your Loved One Dies

Jerome Staten

Introduction

In life, there are a countless amount of trials and tribulations we have to face on a daily basis, in different forms and on its own time frame. Some of these randomly delivered trials and tribulations tend to overwhelm us, leaving us in a frustrated state of mind, wondering if we'll ever get a moment's rest or the elusive breakthrough that we're desperately seeking in life. However, throughout all of the gut wrenching blows that life aggressively stings us with, all of those combined incidents and experiences don't seem to mount up to the devastating annihilation to the heart, mind and soul of losing a loved one. As you're reading this title, be mindful that I'm speaking from the perspective of real life events that I've either experienced within my own life, or circumstances that I'm currently enduring right now. I figured, the same loss and defeats that I've been on the receiving end of, others might be going through the same thing as well and can relate to where I'm coming from. Instead of following through on the advice of some people of me seeking grieving counseling as an attempt to handle the recent loss of my mother to ovarian cancer much better, I find it a bit more relieving to research select topics thoroughly, combine my life experiences with them and deliver it to anyone whose reading this title so you can somewhat get a better understanding of the afterlife as well. I hope you enjoy the information I've provided and if you need to speak with me privately about anything feel free to contact me at the e-mail address I've provided on the title page.

Contents

The Medical System Throws in the Towel

"We've tried multiple forms of chemotherapy, but it's really nothing else left that we can try," my mother's doctor explains, sitting in the frigid hospital room amongst me, my other family members and his team of white jacket wearing followers. "Since this rare form of cancer has been resistant to the chemo treatments we've administered and has obviously spread to other body organs, the only option left at this point is a hospice center or in-home hospice, if that's what you'd prefer."

These words still echo in my head to this very day and I wanted more than anything for my mother to overcome this deadly illness, showing that anything is possible if you just believe. On that particular day, when her doctor requested to speak to my family to explain everything I mentioned about the hospice options, that wasn't good enough for me; I had to remind them that God has the final say. My mother was lying on her hospital bed during this time, somewhat in another world already, either replying with delayed responses when she was awake or showing signs of confusion whenever she was asked questions. Seeing her reach this level was undeniably heartbreaking; my mother was strong willed and extremely active regardless of her situation at one point. It left no doubt in my mind that I had to be her voice now though. The same way she'd praise God's name herself and claim the victory before it was even achieved was the same identical method I had to practice myself , and that's exactly what I did.

Chapter One   The Medical System

Regardless of what the team of doctors had to say, I reminded them time and time again that I believed she'd overcome this battle with ovarian cancer, regardless of the stage it's reached or how badly things presently appeared to be. It didn't take long at all for my decision to be made apparent of what the next phase for my mother would be. Similar to the doctors throwing in the towel, bluntly exclaiming that they couldn't do anything else to save my mother's life, my sister rapidly followed this same trend, confessing that she couldn't do it either, if I chose to bring my mother home to care for her the best way we could with holistic treatments that I researched.

This is the same sister that my mother stood right beside when she went through her battle during her younger days as an adolescent with leukemia. The same sister that had no problem asking for financial assistance constantly in the past from my mother, ultimately causing my mother to be months behind on her bills, but she can't help try to get our mother back on her feet and back to her natural health! My aunt, my mother's sister, was the only one willing to armor up for this battle side-by-side with me. It wasn't going to be easy, but we didn't expect it to be. Being the caregiver for anyone requires an enormous amount of time, patience and understanding all the way through this draining process. The lifestyle you're accustomed to changes drastically when you sign-up to tackle this strenuous dilemma. I didn't care though; I found ways to balance out my time with my kids, the work I had to do, continuously researching different holistic treatments for my mother and then caring for her, with the assistance of my aunt. The nurses that was supposed to come out from the in-home hospice services we signed up for was just as useless to me as my sister was.

To be honest, whenever a member from their staff did show up to ask what medicines or extra supplies my mother needed, I never really picked up on a positive, supportive type of vibe from them that I thought we'd receive. Instead, they'd constantly remind me and my aunt of the final stages of life to look for or ask if funeral arrangements were made; as if they didn't believe that my mother would overcome this battle either. Frustrating doesn't fully describe how I felt at this point, but I'll just go with that term for now.

I felt like I was in the wilderness left all alone to conjure up a vision that no one else around me was actually seeing. My faith was escalated to heights that I'd never imagined it would soar to. People looked at me asking how I was able to remain so calm and confident during one of the scariest times of my family's life. I couldn't explain it, didn't really feel like building up the energy for an explanation that they wouldn't mentally grasp anyway. I just reminded them too that, God would show his face at the perfect time and turn things around for the best. I believed it and no one could tell me differently. Although I was still trying to put the pieces of my spiritual life back together again, after trusting that God would heal my grandmother who had dementia, but eventually died anyway last year, here I stood again, believing that God wouldn't let me down two times in a row by taking my mother as well. Proclaiming that my faith had grown, but having a bit of doubt in the back of my mind, wondering if God would actually give us the victory was too contradictive. If I was going to believe I had to believe wholeheartedly, regardless of how many negative things I heard or how often I had to look into the doubtful faces around me daily.

I submitted my entire trust and belief elements into God's hands and left everything up to him to work it out. All I asked was that he strengthened me as well as my aunt, enabling us to weather this brutal, unpredictable storm until he saw that enough was enough and stepped in to work his wonders. In the beginning stages of this in-home hospice decision of mines, my mother was basically her normal self. In fact, during our brief ride from the hospital to her house that evening when she was discharged, we talked like we'd normally do, no delayed responses or confusion shown on her behalf. Like always, instead of focusing on her life threatening situation at hand, my mother reminded me of her wishes for me to look after my niece (my sister's daughter), making sure she's not from house to house, not having a stable environment to be in. I explained to my mother that night that she still had hope of surviving, and not to focus on other things that would stress her out more than she needed to be. Her doctors explained though that they had disclosed certain information to my mother during her clinic visits that she obviously kept to herself and didn't mention it to me or anyone else in our immediate family. It's probably the reason why my mother felt as though now was the time to remind me to follow up on certain things we discussed in the past; she most likely felt as though her time here on earth was limited at this point.

At home, the protocols I had researched endlessly for were now about to be put to the gruesome test to see if they'd actually do the trick that the traditional western forms of medicines couldn't do. They were natural and organic remedies, but my mother wouldn't try it at first until I used myself as the 'ginnie pig', tasting it to show her that it was harmless.

We laughed about how she could take chemo with no problem, medicines which quite frankly destroys all cells, but she was reluctant to try the natural remedies which really had no significant types of side effects. Seeing me drink the first protocol seemed to ease her mind a bit, leading to her gradually digesting it herself. If this remedy was to work like it did for others that I read about, I knew it wouldn't drastically happen overnight, it would be a timely process. Eating habits had to be revised as well, which quite obviously isn't an overnight success either. When your body is used to digesting certain foods and drinks over the course of the years, depriving it of all of those unhealthy things all of a sudden isn't a walk in the park. You have to gradually lead your body back to a healthy alkalinity level. Most times, when a person has been diagnosed with any form of cancer, this signals off that their body is more acidic than it is alkaline. An acidic body is prone to various diseases and illnesses due to the consumptions of unhealthy foods and drinks. Your immune system becomes weakened at the core, leaving you subject to becoming ill in different ways. Knowing this, my goal was to boost my mother's immune system/alkaline levels, to the healthy range that cancerous cells and/or any other diseases can't thrive in. My time was extremely limited though to pull off this task since the doctors said that the cancer in her body had already began to spread.

At this particular time, due to my mother having an obstruction in her lower bowel, the heavy, solid foods that my mother used to consume regularly wasn't tolerable anymore. She'd eat a small portion every now and then, but the sense of being completely full would surface immediately which caused the usage of softer foods more often.

Chapter One   **The Medical System**

Cereal ranked at the top of my mother's list as one of her most requested foods to eat, but how would I make this work without using the sweet taste of sugar that she loved in her cereal. Doing this, still using sugar in her food and/or drinks, went against the rules of attempting to get her body to the alkaline level it needed to be; cancer thrives off of sugar.

As days went by, no sudden noticeable changes surfaced. My mother's condition didn't improve, but it didn't appear to be getting any worse either. The only difference I saw was, my mother becoming more inclined to being in her bedroom more than any other room of the house. Only one trip downstairs to the dining room was made within a week's time and that long streak continued day after day. However, my mother would sit up on the side of her bed and feed herself or drink whatever beverage she had near her bedside. The nurse from the hospice service still made her brief visits once a week as usual, asking the same questions time and time again, which could've honestly been done over the phone. In my opinion, I believe that it should be some type of median from the point when a patient is discharged from the hospital after the doctors claim it's nothing else that they can do. If more hospitals that claim to have advanced treatments accepted people regardless of what type of medical insurance they may or may not have, more lives would stand a greater chance of being saved. Unfortunately, that's a dream world, far from this world that we currently live in. As far as a median goes, I believe it should be one in place. Some type of spiritual healing combined with holistic treatments, and if all else fails, the hospice services can be used if needed. The reason I say this is, most people from hospice services can only perform whatever lessons they've been taught.

Chapter One   **The Medical System**

From my understanding, their assigned task is to keep the individual as comfortable as possible, mostly with morphine, anxiety meds, etc., while anticipating that death is potentially right around the corner for that person, depending on the condition/circumstance. At least that's what I saw from my perspective. Out of the entire staff that briefly showed up at my mother's house from time to time, I can only recall one young lady even bothering to mention God's name, let alone exemplify a small portion of genuine support to us. Everyone else from their staff watched and anticipated a life ending result, which agitated me tremendously. Here I am, trusting God, having a positive outlook on things, but in return, I still have to hear or see the negativity generating around me. My frustration revealed itself several times without me even parting my lips to mention one word and from that point on, the hospice nurse, social worker and/or staff members, would talk with my aunt privately so they wouldn't be on the receiving end of the annoyed demeanor my facial expressions most likely spewed out to them. I wasn't living in denial, I saw exactly how badly things were, but I still believed that things would get better. I found myself attempting to voice this explanation constantly to these group of doubters who just couldn't see things from my vanish point. So, instead of continuing to do so, I remained focused on the task at hand, anticipating my golden opportunity to prove the theory that I had been preaching all along.

A few more days went by and as the days continued to rapidly venture off, taking its place in history like it's designed to do, an enormous bulk of my mother's strength and energy also appeared to be drifting away within the misty breeze that blew the passing days away from us.

At this point, I was just as reserved as I was before, fully aware that things had the potential of becoming as badly as they could possibly get before we could receive the victory of a stunning turnaround that I believed Christ would grant us with. I can't lie, a bit of uneasiness began to plant itself within my soul, attempting to make me become doubtful, especially when I began to witness my mother communicating with our deceased loved ones as if they were standing before her. I knew that these were the signs of the end of life stages; I had just witnessed my grandmother going through the same phases a year ago. It's also documented within the educational handbook that the in-home hospice services made sure we had a copy of. Even seeing my mother reach this stage, I just knew that God wouldn't let us down. We're supposed to trust in him wholeheartedly, no matter what. Me being the curious type of guy that I am when it comes to the spiritual world, I asked my mother multiple times to explain to me exactly what she was seeing whenever these spiritual forces appeared to her. It seems like, right at the very moment when she'd try to muster up the explanation to give me a crystal clear mental imagery of exactly what she's seeing, she'd blink right back to our earthly realm, describing the clock or picture that's mounted on her bedroom wall. In my opinion, I believe that God made it this way. The only time a person will be able to tell about their after-life spiritual journey is when they're brought back to life completely to do so. Similar to the television show that comes on called 'I Survived . . . Beyond and Back.' This show portrays different people attesting to how things were when they experienced the after-life head on but was eventually sent back to earth because it wasn't their time to die just yet.

However, when a person is going through the transitional stages from life to the spiritual realm, with no point of return, it's almost impossible for them to draw out a picture with words that describes what they're seeing at the exact moment. I mean, you'll know that they're seeing deceased family members, but when it comes to describing how the scenery appears to be, I haven't witnessed this happen yet.

In my mother's case, when she'd snap out of that state of mind, she'd begin talking like her normal self again, picking up from where she left off at with her last unfinished statement that she was previously making. The first thing that came to mind for me was the concern that the cancer may have began to spread to even more organs of her body, despite the different holistic protocols I was administering. It was at this moment when I began to understand why Ovarian Cancer is known as the 'Silent Killer'. By the time a woman realizes that she has this deadly illness, in most cases, it's almost too late to treat it. Knowing that my mother had moments where she'd go in and out of consciousness, I made a pact with her while she was alert, to just continue to trust God first and foremost, and then continue to trust me enough to keep on receiving the protocols I was giving her without being resistant to doing so, if she could help it.

I felt like time was running out for us even faster whenever I saw signs of her condition becoming worse instead of getting better. My mother's alkaline levels still weren't where I needed them to be in order to even attempt to fight off these resistant cancerous cells and at the same time, I'm witnessing her energy level defiantly decreasing right before my eyes. Sitting up on her own on the side of her bed was now a memory.

My mother now required assistance whenever she needed to use the bathroom or just to sit up for a little while to prevent her from lying down so often. When my mother first arrived home from the hospital, I already knew without a doubt that I needed to keep her as active as she used to be. This was somewhat of a Catch -22 though because even though I needed to keep my mother active, allowing her muscles to remain flexible and at the same time allow the oxygen to continuously circulate within her system as a result of getting a sufficient amount of daily exercise, the chemotherapy and cancerous cells had already taken it's toll on my mother's immune system. Just as much as cancer cells love sugar, it also thrives and spreads even faster in a body that's inactive.

Now I'm stuck between a rock and a hard place, almost on the verge of having to witness my mother deteriorate daily. As if this wasn't bad enough, my aunt and I were now being limited on the supplies we requested from the hospice service. I tell you, by this being my first time stepping into the role of being a caregiver; I got the opportunity to see firsthand how much of a headache our system can really be. Things work so much easier when you're dealing with a team of people who really care, living up to their job descriptions to the fullest. Whenever you're dealing with people who are in their field of work strictly for the paycheck, regardless of how small it may actually be, you'll receive the mediocre type of services like me and my aunt received dealing with this hospice company. To put the icing on the cake, they actually have the nerve to send out a survey or have a representative call to find out if you're satisfied with the services they're providing. I honestly hope I never have to go through this draining process again.

On my ride home that rainy evening, I recall just taking this timely journey in complete silence, no radio playing, no anything. In doing so, I was creating the one-on-one uninterrupted dialog with God that I set out to make a habit of doing on a regular basis. We're taught not to question God because everything he does or allows to happen is done so with a purpose that we can't mentally grasp most times. Even still, I had the burning desire to ask, "God, where are you?" I was doing everything possible that I could humanly do to save my mother's life, but I saw things going in the opposite direction of how I pictured them turning out to be. While I'm still researching different protocols, living up to my assignment of figuring out how to do my part physically as far as finding ways to tackle this resistant cancer, trusting God to handle things spiritually, my sister spent her time visiting Facebook, posting several false, attention seeking comments on her wall, consisting of bogus information about what she's doing for my mother. Those who saw and knew differently brought it to my attention, but I refused to stoop to my sister's level by posting the truth as a response to each remark that she was falsely documenting. Besides, when my aunt did just that, she all of a sudden became deleted as one of my sister's friends on Facebook, because the truth was being revealed to those who was interested enough to read it.

Nevertheless, tons of prayers continuously poured in from various places; family, friends, my mother's church and prayer group, etc.

Any other time, when my mother was fully aware of the amount of support she was receiving from so many people, she'd become emotional as a result, teary-eyed when she explained how happy and motivated this made her feel. This motivation is what sparked up the flames for my mother to flat out tell each doctor who treated her condition in the past that, she'd overcome this cancer battle, and eventually walk back into the hospital one day on her own power, cancer-free. Unfortunately, this wasn't the case temporarily. My mother's health was still declining and half the time by her being so incoherent, she rarely responded verbally when told that the same prayers that used to excite her at one point were still flowing in. This was a major devastation to me mentally, physiological and spiritually, but I still believed. I believed so much because I know what God is capable of doing, if it's his Will.

Besides, my mother requested for me to stick with her and that's exactly what I intended to do. I repeatedly coached her on, explaining to never give up, just keep praying, even when I had to whisper it into her ear with no verbal response sometimes. I knew my mother could hear me, but I was praying that God was listening to our cry for help as well. By it being just me and my aunt taking care of my mother, we'd rotate our schedules to the best of our ability. Whenever I'd leave out in the evening, my aunt would come in to stay the night, or vice-versa. During the times when I didn't stay the night, coming to my mother's house the following morning left me in a predicament where as though I didn't know what to expect to see or what report my aunt would have for me.

Chapter Two   God, Where Are You?

Some days, I'd come into my mother's house and my mother would be sitting up, getting bathed, eating the little bit that she could eat or waiting for the sheets on her bed to be changed. Then there are times when I'd come into her bedroom to witness my mother sleeping the majority of the day, briefly responding to whatever I said to her whenever she was awake. Anyone who's familiar with this knows that excessive sleeping for a terminally ill person is another sign that the end of life might be getting nearer for that individual. For me, I didn't dismiss the fact that my mother could've been depressed as well, which caused her to sleep so much. Deep depression is another battle within itself that also has excessive sleeping as one of its symptoms. Either way, giving my mother the protocols I was using was becoming strenuous because she wasn't awake long enough to digest it. I went from using a normal sized cup to using the plastic dropper that came with the morphine in order for me to squeeze the recommended amount of my cancer fighting protocol into my mother's mouth. My mother would swallow it with no problem, but I could tell that her body was beginning to shut down and it was just a matter of time before she wouldn't accept anything at all if things continued down this pathway.

I can remember sitting at my mother's bedside on several occasion, almost scratching a hole in my head, wondering what more I could possibly do that I wasn't already doing to help her. It was during these overwhelming moments of mines when Satan would always find a way to creep his way into my overly stressed brain, taunting me with the thought that God doesn't acknowledge my humble cry. On the other hand, I knew that God heard me loud and clear.

The only thing I couldn't comprehend was, why I didn't see any physical improvements yet when it came to my mother's health. As an added incentive to prove the medical system wrong, whom explained to my mother, as well as me and my family that they only expected her to live for another couple of weeks when she was discharged from the hospital, I held onto that discharge sheet, constantly glancing at how her doctor checked 'NO' all the way down the paper when it came to resuscitation. Holding onto it was motivation for me. I wanted more than anything to prove that God has the final say, regardless of how many medical degrees they may have or how often they've seen things result in the manner that they've predicted it would end with other patients. So, instead of ripping that particular piece of paper up, tossing it in the trashcan like the first nurse that came out suggested that I should do after she revised it like I requested, checking 'YES' all the way down the sheet, I just held onto it. In my mind, when my mother's health improved dramatically, enough for her to follow up on her prediction of walking back into that hospital one day, cancer-free, I wanted to be right beside her with this piece of paper in hand to give it right back to the doctor who checked 'NO' for everything.

Unfortunately, seeing my mother waving one morning toward an empty area above her wardrobe, speaking excitedly to my grandfather (her father), who passed away almost 30 years ago, made me aware that the image I had in my head of us walking back into the hospital together with the victory, was further off than I'd hope it would be. Her father wasn't the only deceased loved one my mother saw that day. She also saw my uncle who passed away from throat cancer almost 12 years ago.

The way my mother pointed toward her ceiling, as if she was trying to keep up with my uncle's active movement, caused me to draw the conclusion that my uncle must have had wings and was flying around right before my mother's eyes. All within a day's time, I witnessed my mother speak to her deceased father, to pointing in various areas of her bedroom trying to get me to see my deceased uncle who was obviously flying around, concluding with her looking over on the floor bedside her bed in search of my grandmother who was most likely hiding from her. The brief opportunity I had of having my mother receive the protocols I was giving her while she was still somewhat fully aware of what was going on without being confused, was snatched out of my possession at a rapid pace. Things appeared to be on the verge of beginning to make the positive turnaround that I was praying for at one point, just to decline twice as fast as it did when she was in the hospital, as time went by.

The patience I once had of Noah from the Bible was beginning to wear thin. I began to scramble with the dilemma in my head, wondering if I should discontinue the hospice service just to enable my mother the opportunity to go back to the hospital for at least a blood transfusion. The hospice service wouldn't administer this and I wasn't sure if my mother's blood level was low, if she needed an I-V because of her fluid intake being low as well, or I had just run out of time and options all together. All I know is, things weren't looking good at all and for the very first time, I could see it myself now. My mother had become completely unresponsive verbally. She'd wink her eyes or moan whenever my aunt and I attempted to get her more comfortable in bed, but that's about it.

All I kept thinking to myself was, I hope I'm not getting closer to the point of having to witness my mother pass away. I mean, I know age doesn't make a difference, but she's only 48-years-old and we're both trusting God with every fiber of our being; things couldn't be on the verge of ending like this.

The next morning wasn't any better. We had to eventually call the hospice nurse to come out because my mother's breathing pattern began to change. The calm inhale and exhale motion that a human being usually displays changed into a struggle to breathe type of motion in my mother's case. This resulted in an oxygen machine being brought out to help my mother breathe better. Family members and friends could obviously sense that we were running out of time as well because my mother's room was full of visitors on that particular day, mostly all day long. We all just sat around exchanging thoughts about the various amount of things that's going on in our world today and how the Bible foretold these end-time events as they seem to be unfolding day-by-day. Throughout these prolonged interesting conversations, we made sure we monitored my mother's blood pressure range, which had dropped extremely low earlier that morning, but went back up a little bit off and on. The hospice nurse recommended that we didn't worry so much about the blood pressure readings, but instead focus on my mother's breathing pattern and any new signs that may appear as the day went on. I lie to you not, it seemed like as soon as the nurse explained different things to observe, (a skin discoloration, any sores or bumps, etc) one of these things appeared later that night when everyone was gone home for the evening.

Chapter Two   **God, Where Are You?**

I had even made it home myself until my aunt called, explaining that my mother's breathing was even worse now and how the bottom of my mother's foot, on her heel area, turned a purplish-red color. In a matter of minutes, I slipped on some clothes and headed back to my mother's house to see what my aunt was referring to. It didn't take long for me to see how my mother's breathing had changed when I arrived. It appeared as if my mother was almost choking now, trying to take the same breathes that was once normal to her. Enough was enough at this point for my aunt. The emotions that were consumed inside of her all along busted out forcefully, as she flopped down next to my mother on the bed, crying her heart out, explaining how sorry she was that my mother had to suffer so much. While my aunt is positioned beside my mother on the bed at this point, I'm hovering over top of my mother, making her aware that I'm still with her as well like I promised I'd be. I knew she was unable to verbally respond, but I also knew that she could hear me loud and clear. The reason I know my mother could hear me is because just a few seconds after I told her that she fought long and hard and I explained how much we love her, I literally looked into my mother's eyes and witnessed her take her final breath. It was like she was actually waiting on me to release her.

A major part of me left this earth at that very moment as well when I actually saw the look in my mother's eyes when she passed away. My mother's eyes were teary, almost as if she wanted to say so much before passing away but just couldn't do so. However, she also had a peaceful look as well, showing no signs of fear when at one point in time, my mother was a woman who was afraid to die.

After I took time to think about it, I understood better how she was able to transcend without being afraid any more. My mother wasn't even in anymore pain right before she passed and this was obvious because she refused the morphine to ease her pain. A combination of God, my mother's Guardian Angels and my other deceased family members whom my mother saw, comforted my mother on her journey from earth to the spiritual realm. In doing so, my mother didn't feel any more pain or didn't have anything else to be fearful of any longer, she was free. I realized these things after the fact, but before I thought about it, right when my mother took her final breath, I was honestly furious, pissed off that I believed so much just to be let down yet again. I can remember pacing back and forth throughout the house that night, verbally expressing my frustration, anger and disappointment openly. The loud cries from my family members mourning my mother's passing was the only thing outweighing the sound of my verbal disturbance brewing up from the depths of my pain ridden soul. When Satan appeared this time, it was a swift visit just to ask me, "Where's Your God Now?" For me, I believe I went through every emotion a human being can possibly go through all in one night. The same woman, who gave me life, carried me for nine months in her stomach and would do anything under the sun to assist me throughout my years as a kid growing up, is now the same woman I'm helping the mortician carry out of her house in a body bag. I was literally out of my body at this point, the out-of-body experience you might hear people refer to at times. I gave every ounce of energy, time and dedication I had to offer, just to witness things end in a way that I prayed consistently that I would never have to experience again.

Chapter Two

God, Where Are You?

Funeral arrangements now have to be made, I have to watch my mother be buried six feet underneath the dirt just like I witnessed with my grandmother a year ago and on top of that the doctors win with their prediction. My ride back to my house that night was a total blur. I just couldn't believe that my mother was no longer on this planet any longer, when she was just alive a few minutes ago. Heart-wrenching to the third degree is the only way I can describe it.

The scenery ended just like it began, with just three people in my mother's room that night. Me, my aunt and my mother, giving it all we had while trusting in God. Other family members arrived and returned back again that evening after finding out that my mother had passed away, but when this transition was actually occurring, it was just me, my aunt and my mother in the room. My mother trusted me and my aunt enough to literally place her life into our hands until God intervened with his decision of what should happen next. I obviously didn't sleep a wink that night and it really didn't hit me until the following day that I had lost my mother. I guess I was hoping that it was all just a horrible nightmare that I'd eventually wake up from, but reality slapped me dead across the face to awaken me to a new day that I just didn't have the energy to face. I crumbled underneath the piercing annihilation of my misery and pain the following morning. My appetite was nowhere to be found, a huge shock wave was unleashed on the faith that I had worked so hard and long to build up. Like I stated before, I didn't even get a chance to get over the loss of my grandmother and now I have to digest and live with the stunning fact that my mother isn't physically here anymore either.

To this very day, thoughts reflect endlessly in my mind of several things I witnessed during my mother's end-of- life stages. I can just image the look my mother had on her face one night when my aunt explained to her that I was trying different things to help save her life. My aunt told me that when she said this to my mother, my mother glanced at her and excitedly asked, "Am I going to live?" I felt like it was my job and my duty to give my mother all I had, win-lose-or draw. True, I did feel defeated when I saw that giving my all still wasn't enough, but when my mother winked at me that night, right before I told her we love her and she took her final breath, I saw an imagery of victory written all over her face. Then in my grandmother's case, with her battling with dementia, I still remember her praising God, singing religious songs and shouting openly in the hospital on several occasions, regardless of how badly her mind had become. In both scenarios, with my mother and grandmother, I also saw them both return to their child-like stages at some point.

My mother and other deceased family members aren't here physically anymore, but now is my time to share with you how they're still here spiritually. If you've loss anyone who's close to you and you're wondering what happens after they've transcended to the spiritual-realm after life here on earth, the next few chapters will explain this to you in full detail. Although nothing can possibly replace the void in a person's life of losing people who are near and dear to the heart, me personally, I find just a slight bit of comfort knowing that my deceased loved ones are still capable of looking over me. All because you can't visibly see the people who may have passed away that were close to you, doesn't mean that they're not right there with you.

The Transition from Earth to the Spiritual Realm

First and foremost, before we go into full detail about the Spiritual Realm, one must believe that Jesus Christ walked the face of this earth, was crucified but, rose from his death to be transcended into Heaven. If you don't accept the fact that Christ is the Father, Son and the Holy Spirit (Trinity), read no further. However, if you are a believer and you're interested to know more about the Spiritual Realm then I invite you to continue on with the information provided within this book. Often times, you'll come across people in your daily life who doesn't completely understand the elements required when it comes to the entire creation of the human anatomy. We acknowledge the fact that we're physical beings with a soul, but some forget that we also have a spirit that's intact with our physical being as well. Think about it. If this wasn't so, how could we be created in the image of God? While the soul and spirit are so closely related, it can be extremely difficult at times to distinguish the difference. The word "spirit" when used in the Scriptures has several meanings. Whenever the word "Spirit" appears used with a capital letter, it has but one meaning. It is the name of the third Person of the Trinity, Holy Spirit of God. The word "spirit" spelled with a small letter may have one of several different meanings. It can have direct reference to the spirit of man which is as much a part of the tripartite nature of man as the Spirit of the living God is a Person of the Holy Trinity. Or it can indicate an evil spirit such as any agent of the Devil.

We will confine ourselves here to the Biblical usage of the word only as it relates to the spirit of man, one of the three constituent parts of his being. In his unfallen state the 'Spirit' of man was illuminated from Heaven, but when the human race fell in Adam, sin closed the window of the Spirit, pulled down the curtain, and the chamber of the spirit became a death chamber and remains so in every unregenerate heart, until the Life and Light giving power of the Holy Spirit floods that chamber with the Life and Light giving power of the new life in Christ Jesus. It develops then that the spirit of man, being the sphere of God-consciousness, is the inner or private office of man where the work of regeneration takes place. When it comes to the soul, a human being not only has a living soul but we are a living soul. The Bible says: "And the Lord God formed man of the dust of the ground, and breathed into his nostrils the breath of life, and man became a living soul" (Genesis 2:7). We must be careful not to confound that which is truly spiritual and that which is merely soulish or psychical. We have seen that the spirit of man is the sphere of activity where the Holy Spirit operates in regeneration. Just so is the soul the sphere of activity where Satan operates making his appeal to the affections and emotions of man.

Satan knows full well that he dominates the psychical or the soulish man. Therefore he does not care if a man goes to a church where the Spirit of God is not in evidence. He knows that his victim is a creature of emotions, and it matters not if the emotions are stirred to sentimentalism or even to tears, just so long as man's spirit does not come in contact with God's Holy Spirit. Personally, I believe that Satan would rather have a man go to a modernistic church where there is false worship than he would have him go to a house of prostitution.

The soul is the seat of the passions, the feelings, and the desires of man; and Satan is satisfied if he can master these. When you think about it, how man (Adam) was created from dust, having the breath of life breathed into his nostrils to make him become a living soul, this is the same dust one must return to after death, enabling the soul to rest until Christ returns. Although the soul is at rest at this point, keep in mind that the Spirit is still alive and active even after it transcends from our human body. Although we're unable to visibly see these human spirits with our naked eyes, don't be mistaken and assume that they don't exist, because they do. This is the reason why I started off this chapter by mentioning Christ and how he transcended from his death into the Spiritual Realm. By doing so, it enables us as humans to do the same after our time here on the Earth has come to an end. When Christ returns for the Second Coming, those whom are dead in Christ (the deceased who accepted Christ as their Savior) will rise first to meet him in the air, followed by those who may still be alive here on earth. It's at this point when the human soul and spirit will be united with a new, glorified body.

If you've ever been in the presence of a loved one, or anyone else for this matter, when they're experiencing the end-of- life stages, you'll notice them calling out for people who are already deceased or talking to them as if they're standing right in front of them. They're entering the Spiritual Realm, enabling them to see these people even though we can't see them ourselves. These spirits appear as an assistance to help the person who's dying cross over more comfortably. In my opinion, it's the unknown, not knowing what to expect in the after-life that causes so many people to be afraid of death.

This transition is made a bit easier when you see people you recognize (deceased spirits), that'll help you transcend to the next dimension. From my understanding, your Guardian Angel will greet you as well, explaining who they are and what their assignment is when it comes to you, but, seeing your family members (even if they are deceased spirits), seems to bring more comfort to those who are passing away. After your time here on Earth has ended and you've transcended into the Spiritual Realm, expect to eventually undergo a life review. This process is done to show you different things you've done within the course of your life and how you could've handled certain situations much better but, you won't be judged just yet. The judgment only occurs when Christ returns for the Second Coming.

Nevertheless, the Spiritual Realm consists of two major dimensions which are; Spiritual Paradise (Heaven) and Spiritual Prison (Hell), which is both temporary until Christ returns and decides where you'll be for eternity. Those who are in Spiritual Paradise will preach the gospel to those who are in Spiritual Prison, still providing an opened door for those whom are in Hell to accept the gospel and accept Christ, resulting in their opportunity to enter Paradise as well. However, not every spirit, once it leaves the human body, is willing to cross over into the Spiritual Realm. Some choose to remain earthbound, attempting to look after their loved ones who are still alive, who may be grieving tremendously, having a difficult time accepting that their loved one has passed away.

Then there are some spirits who cause chaos even from the Spiritual World. For instance, a person may move into the very home that this deceased person once owned or resided in and, that might not set well with the person who's deceased. They're capable of doing multiple things as an attempt to run this person away from that particular residence. It may have been an incident already where as though you've been home alone and, you may have heard noises but didn't have a clue of where the noises were coming from. I experienced this myself in the past and the sound was so evident it caused me to look around near the staircase of my hallway to see if I actually saw someone walking up and down the steps, which I didn't. Again, whatever you do, never underestimate the power of spirits just because they're not visible to you. Some are capable of knocking things over, flicking a light switch, or causing the confusing noises and crackling sounds I just mentioned. The Spiritual Realm is a real world, invisible to the natural eye but visible to the eye of faith. In fact, long before the physical universe even existed, the spiritual universe was already in place.

This Realm consists of Angels who are currently invisible to us as humans. From my studies, I've noticed that the Bible doesn't reveal the names of many Angels, but it does mention the names of three members of the Angelic Realm known as archangels. God administered his government through these three archangels named Gabriel, Michael and Lucifer.

These archangels are mentioned throughout the Bible, but one archangel in particular is the key to understanding our current world events and to solving an important paradox. The Bible can very well be synonymous to a jig saw puzzle. Many will read this same material and draw their own conclusions from it as they're attempting to put the pieces of the puzzle together to understand the true meaning of the texts. In order to solve the mystery of this jig saw puzzle, one must combine the clues made available in the Old and the New Testaments. According to the genealogical records of the Bible, from the time of Adam to our present day is less than 6,000 years. An apparent paradox exists if one is to believe God created the Heavens and the Earth around 6,000 years ago; while science suggests that the Earth is billions of years old. A main clue lies in a letter written by John the Apostle during the time he was exiled on the Island of Patmos.

Revelation is the name of this book, the account of a vision God used to reveal important information to John about the end time. The reason I'm mentioning the book of Revelation is because this is the book that Angels play an important role in, being involved with God's judgments upon Earth. The difficulty we face lies in being able to comprehend the connection and relationships between God, the things of this world (Earthly Realm) and what's going on in the after-life (Spiritual Realm). Keep in mind, the term 'angel' means messenger or worker who is sent to bring about God's presence by carrying out his Will.

Having said this, one must be mindful that even the bad angels
(demons) are subject to the Will of God and serve his purpose
also. Angels can manifest themselves in a number of forms. For
the most part they operate sight unseen in a separate dimension
but can also cross over to this dimension that we live in. Both
good and evil angels can take on human form and closely
interact with us. It's extremely important to study the history of
angels and how they operate so you'll understand that it is
indeed another dimension after life here on Earth (Spiritual
World) that we as humans transcend to after death. While the
spirit our loved ones who have passed away can still
acknowledge our emotions, grief, etc, there are also instances
where as though one can visit the Spiritual World as well. This is
mostly done within our dreams when we sleep at night. In my
case, I'd pray for certain things extensively, asking God to reveal
the answers to me and most times, it was done so while I was
asleep, in my dreams.

The same can apply to deceased loved ones. They're capable of
communicating with us in multiple forms; in our dreams is one
effective way of doing so. You may or may not realize this but,
every night when we are asleep; we actually visit the spiritual
world briefly, especially when we are in a deep sleep and is in
what is known as 'delta wave.' Most of us don't recall our visit
to the Spiritual World after we've awakened, and then there are
those who can precisely remember step-by-step what occurred
within their dreams/nightmares.

The nights when we have a good night's sleep, including times
when there are no dreams at all, most of us will wake up feeling
thoroughly refreshed, which indicates that our energy level has
been recharged in the astral. If we dream about someone who
died and this person appears to be in their prime or even younger
years, this is the surest sign that we are in the astral.
Furthermore, when we're about to die our energy levels become
lower and lower and, our consciousness levels go in and out of
our physical bodies. This is when the spirit leaves the body
intermittently. This pattern gradually continues until the final
departure, when the silver cord is served. This 'silver cord' I'm
mentioning connects the spiritual body to the physical body and,
when the cord is finally served, all the subtle body's involutes
and aggregate at the heart chakra. To the clairvoyant eyes a light
is seen hovering over the heart chakra. Then after a short while
the total spirit with all its attendant bodies will depart from the
physical body through the 7th chakra, at the top of the head
where the anterior fontanel used to be. While the spirit is
congregating at the heart chakra, life will slowly withdraw from
the body, starting at the toes and feet. This paralysis will slowly
move up to the legs, thighs and then the torso area, resulting in
the final total paralysis coinciding with the withdrawal of the
spirit from the body. Just like I previously mentioned about my
mother's face having an appearance of complete calmness and
peace, this is the final stage that's reached once the spirit has
fully transcended from the body.

Now, once the spirit has completely left the body, leaving the corpse for good, several things is bound to occur. Again, in my mother's case, she was immediately met by deceased family members. In other scenarios, some spirits are quickly met by spiritual guides to help them cross over. After some greetings and catching up of events, the individual is then led away by the spiritual guides to a place for a rest. In cases where the individual has suffered from an illness for a long time here on earth, he/she will be sent to a convalescent home for a prolonged rest and healing. Now remember, I mentioned praying that God would heal my mother and he did so, just not for this world. Even if we don't get to see our loved ones become healed here on earth, just be mindful that they are healed in the Spiritual World. If they're in Spiritual Paradise, the suffering, agony and pain that they endured here on earth is a thing of the past, they're free from that now. This is another thing that brings comfort to me, helping me to continue to push forward in life after experiencing two devastating losses back to back. Just knowing that my mother and grandmother is pain free but are still capable of watching over me helps a lot and, I hope that whoever reads this, can find comfort in knowing that your deceased loved one is doing the same for you. As far as the journey one must take when entering the Spiritual Realm, some, on the other hand, will either go through a dark tunnel or climb up a flight of stairs toward the bright light, where deceased family members and/or friends will happily greet this individual, explaining the situation at hand.

After going through this phase and then experiencing the life review segment, the individual will then be taken to the Realm where he/she has earned the right to reside. The Realm where the individual will reside entirely depends on how the individual performed here on earth throughout their life. During this period, the individual's spiritual guide will look after them and this may occur for some time. Another thing to be mindful of is, we're all programmed to have a date and time of distinction; although none of us know the exact day and time when we'll pass away. For those who are murdered or may commit suicide, after death, these spirits are confused due to the simple fact that their life was ended prematurely than originally programmed. In fact, these individuals won't even realize right away that their dead. These individuals will see or hear their loved ones mourning and crying over the deceased corpse but, when trying to verbally convince their loved ones that they're alright, it won't work because their loved ones won't even hear them.

This scenario will continuously repeat itself until reality finally sinks in for this individual that they're actually dead. Regardless of the life ending circumstance, being the situation where the person understands that they've passed on, or when murder or suicide occurs causing the spirit to be in a confused state, as I stated before, some spirits still remain earth bound for a long period of time.

As earlier mentioned, these spirits that decide to remain earth bound are the ones who are very attached to their families, their homes, their businesses, or are just afraid of what lies on the other side for them. To those who are able to see them, these earth bound spirits will appear as ghost. Think for a brief moment of how it must feel to first transcend from your body as just a spirit, glancing down at your deceased corpse regardless of the scene where this may have unfolded. You see things exactly how they are on earth but, even if you're speaking as loudly as you possibly can, attempting to continue to hold a dialogue with your family members and friends, they're unable to hear a word that you're saying. On top of that, they can't even see you. All they see is your corpse that's lying before them as they're weeping over you. Sounds like a scene from a movie doesn't it? In reality, this is very real and it happens every time a person dies and their spirit leaves the physical body. The spiritual world is composed of innumerable interpenetrating realms around the physical world. It's not geographically far away or way up from the earth, but it is interpenetrating and just around us.

Growing up, I used to be confused whenever I'd often times hear people using the phrase, "To be absent from the body is to be present with the Lord." The confusion with me came from me knowing that the soul sleeps when death occurs; however, I left out the spirit element which explains this phrase much better. These are the elements of the Human Trinity that I also mentioned earlier: (Body, Soul, and Spirit).

Energy also plays a huge part in all of this as well because it's undoubtedly what everything is made of. Energy is just the vibration force that your spirit is evolving at during any given moment.

As a spirit, you begin to move into energy levels of vibration which are words that you hear about on earth very often - - harmony, forgiveness, compassion, etc. As a spirit you are moving into becoming all of these things combined. When doing so, you're beginning to move into your own higher spiritual being. From my studies, spirits have a great connection with their loved ones here on earth. However, they do not sit and continuously watch the events taking place in the lives of each one of their loved ones as its happening. They have a very telepathic way of knowing when big events are taking place, when their loved ones are celebrating or in distress. They also can have this telepathic connection with several family members throughout the world at the same time and are aware of what is taking place in each loved-one's life.

The Law of Homogeneity is what prevents humans from seeing a spirit. The spirit is of a finer essence than the soul, because, in contrast to the soul, the spirit is non-material. In appearance, it is similar; it looks like a man or a woman but has a much more beautiful, radiant and perfect form than man or soul.

We already know that the soul is of ethereal matter, that's why it lives longer than the body which is made of gross matter, but it also will eventually expire. The spirit, being non-material, will never expire, it is eternal. As soon as, in the Spiritual Realm, the desire for an individual personality is awoken in the spirit-germ, it works in a subconscious way towards this goal, i.e., starts seeking the right conditions. Until the longing life has awakened, it was immobile, seemingly sleeping. The volition for development is the first movement of the spirit. Under the influence of the Law of Motion and the Law of Gravity, the spirit-germ starts to sink from the Spiritual Realm into the lower spheres in order to develop. It stops at the edge of the Ethereal World. Here, under certain conditions, the outer shell starts to form, first into the shape of a child that gradually grows and develops into an adult. That way, in the Ethereal World, the soul forms into a human shape, representing the cover of the spirit-germ.

The spirit-germ in the nucleus of the soul remains undeveloped. Similarly, while, from an apple no apple can grow without a tree, people also have to develop a soul first, only thereafter the spirit. That's why the Ethereal World emerged earlier, in order for the souls to develop first. Only after, they developed, after a human form has been achieved, the World of Matter and the Earth, where souls enter physical bodies, arose. The whole of the gross material Universe has one purpose only - it serves the development of spirit-germs.

The stay in the Ethereal World is only a transitory period needed
for the formation of the soul - the covering of the spirit. The soul
is, in fact, a connection, an intermediary, with the help of which
the spirit-germ connects with the body in order to be able to
function on Earth, and thereby develop. The body protects the
soul and spirit as well, from the coarse influences of the
environment. In the Spiritual Realm, in the middle part, which is
called "Paradise" or, according to the Bible "God's Kingdom",
the Developed Spirit lives as a male or female being. In Paradise,
unlike in the Material Worlds, evil or imperfection no longer
exists. Here, is only beauty, love, goodness and justice rule, but
not inactivity. The Law of Motion is valid for all levels of
Creation. The blissfulness of spirits does not stem from
being passive but from a joyful, creative and well organized
activity. The purpose of the life of all Developed Spirits is,
among other things, to help other so far undeveloped spirits -
people in the World of Matter, to finish their development on
time and return as mature spirits to their home.

In Paradise, there also live children of different ages, but they are
not born as here, on Earth; they do not have parents; they belong
to everyone. They also arose from the spirit-germs. They
immediately formed in this level - as children. They need not
sink into the World of Matter for development, as they are
perfect right away. They lack maturity which they will reach
gradually through contact with Developed Spirits.

Chapter Three   **The Transition From Earth**

And so, life in Paradise is varied: there are male, female, and child spirits and every one of them can experience emotions. All spirits are active in some way. Fatigue or stress does not exist in Paradise because they are only the manifestation of matter. The fact that there is daylight around the clock and that light here is much brighter than on Earth also contributes to a joyful life and constant activity. There is no trace of darkness or evil.

Perfect spirits, although they have free will, will never choose the path of doubting, distortion or evil. Their intuitive sensing, behavior and deeds are not a matter of choosing between good and evil, as they are pure and clear. Imperfect spirits, owing to free will, will often choose even wrong paths, as they want to experience them. Regretfully, these are not always a lesson for them. Frequently they take them away from the real goal, even if they do not realize it. It is because of this imperfection that spirit-germs of human spirits cannot form in the Spiritual Realm, because the Law of Homogeneity does not allow it. Satan fights hard to keep our 'eye of faith' closed and blinded. The eye of faith that I'm referring to doesn't just consist of being able to conceive the Spiritual Realm, but it also includes being able to exercise our senses to hear and feel things that are occurring in the Spiritual Realm as well. Satan does everything in his power to prevent this from happening. A person who is not saved and doesn't believe in Christ to begin with, can't grasp this invisible Realm that I'm speaking of. These human beings are limited to their senses alone in which they operate in.

We are able to be sure of what we hope for when we realize it already exists with God in the spiritual realm. The promises of God make us aware of what God has provided for us. Our study and reading of the Bible (with the expressed aid of the Holy Spirit, because even the Word of God is without proper understanding without Him) will increase our faith and cause us to have a better understanding of what God has made available for us in the spiritual realm. Faith comes by hearing and hearing and hearing and hearing (hearing aloud and hearing with the eyes) the Word of God.

Another thing to be mindful of is an animal's ability to be able to sense the spirit of a person who's deceased. While it may be safe to say that several animals ability to sense things are way stronger than a human being senses might be, I'm going to use a cat in this situation, because again, this is something I've witnessed with my mother's cat. Even before my mother passed away, I'd say right around the time when she came home from the hospital, my mother's cat became more attached to her than she normally would be. When I say attached, I mean remaining in my mother's room, either lying underneath or even beside my mother's bed the maturity of the time. My mother's cat would cry loudly at night, almost resembling the sound of a baby, even though she wasn't hungry, thirsty or anything of that nature. It was as if she could sense my mother's illness and maybe even more than that for all I know.

Most times when people come around that cats aren't used to seeing, some of them will run into the next room or hide underneath the bed or something. My mother's cat refused to leave my mother's presence regardless of the amount of visitors who were making their way into my mother's bedroom to visit her. When I think about it, the only time my mother's cat would leave the room was only when she needed to eat or use her litter box. Other than that, she remained in my mother's presence. Now that my mother has passed away, her cat still shows signs of depression and believe it or not, she still prefers to be in my mother's bedroom opposed to any other room of the house. I can't speak about other animals because I'm not certain but, when it comes to cats, they have a heightened awareness of spiritual energy.

Any true observer of animals (cats in particular) will know that what some might call beasts are actually intelligent creatures, adept at communicating without language. Somehow, cats apparently share a connection with each other that is perhaps best described as a form of psychic energy. It's this form of the sixth sense that possibly allows cats, as well as other animals, to be more in-tune with the invisible world way more effectively than a human being is capable of doing. If you have a cat, pay close attention to how they may focus their attention on something, or even run and/or jump at it without you being able to visibly see with your own eyes the very thing that's attracting them so much.

Animals are way smarter than some humans give them credit for being. A recent study shows that cat senses are 80% more powerful than a human being. The reason being is because cats are descendants of predators, and still operate as such. Cats seem to possess an elevated level for emotion and empathy toward humans and even other animals for that matter, which explains how they're able to sense when their owner is distressed or ill. Cats grieve and mourn over the loss of a close human companion just like we do as humans. The death or absence may change an established hierarchy as well as being the absence of a familiar companion. While this is not the ritualized grief of humans, the sudden absence of something familiar is distressing to many cats.

In the context of bereavement, this stress is termed grief. The major difference between human and feline grief is that cats grieve for familiar and close companions while humans show grief for a distant relative or for a public figure. Cats lack the abstraction (and the memory capacity) that allows humans to grieve for someone we have never met or who has been absent from our life for a prolonged period of time. Humans often have elaborate or ritualized ways of dealing with their grief. Cats may become withdrawn or, at the other extreme, over-attached and "clingy". Humans understand grief as being the sense of loss following a death. It is a form of anxiety felt at the abrupt severing of a relationship or the sudden absence of a familiar person. Cats react to this sudden absence as well and therefore, may show anxiety or grief in situations such as this too.

The Toll That Death Has On Kids

The emotional devastation of losing a loved one is a dreadful dilemma that overwhelms all parties involved. I've mentioned the toll it's taken on me of losing both my mother and grandmother almost a year apart, and I've also described how this sudden absence can affect animals as well. Above anything else, how does a child come to grips with dealing with this sudden loss themselves? When it comes to my kids, both of my sons, as well as my daughter are still feeling the physical absence of their grandmother (my mother) in their lives to this very day. The same way I had to receive the brutal blow to my entire physical being of losing these two women who are near and dear to my heart, is the same emotional experience my kids have to endure because of how close my immediate family is. It's not a good feeling for anyone involved, regardless of which angle a person may analyze things from. It hurts to the core and those who've never experienced a loss of this magnitude can never fully understand how it feels to go through it.

They can always offer their sympathy and support but, that's where the buck stops. These people can only imagine how you're feeling but, that's about it. It's not a piece of cake for an adult to weather this storm so you can just imagine the toll it obviously takes on a child.

Chapter Four   The Toll That Death Has On Kids

My oldest son, who is a teenager now, stood by my mother's bedside one morning, praying and begging that she'd get better, exclaiming how he wouldn't be ok without her. My mother was verbally unresponsive at this time and I explained to my son that she could still hear him even if she's wasn't replying. Like most grandmother's, my mother somewhat spoiled my kids by trying to get them whatever they may have requested, that was a reasonable price. When my mother explained to people outside of the family that she'd go through a blaze of fire for her family, that wasn't an understatement by a long shot, which is why I had to give her my all, especially when she needed it the most. Knowing this sudden loss would cause temporary mental and physical disturbance, I allowed my kids to miss a couple of days from school so they wouldn't have to sit amongst their peers with their hearts filled with this much pain.

As I stated earlier, as strong as I am, I couldn't even pull myself out of bed to face the world the following morning after seeing my mother die the night before so, I wouldn't dare force my kids to do so. Their grief was apparently just as equivalent as mines. Nevertheless, the best way, well, really the only way I know how to assist my kids with overcoming this kind of obstacle is by always having an opened line of communication with them. They're able to ask me anything and in exchange, I'll explain things honestly to them so they'll get somewhat of a better understanding. My daughter is younger than my two sons, which requires me to explain things to her a little differently.

Chapter Four   **The Toll That Death Has On Kids**

Until kids are about 5 or 6 years old, their view of the world is very literal. So explaining the death in basic and concrete terms is the approach I've taken. Now, as kids mature into teens, they start to understand that every human being eventually dies, regardless of grades, behavior, wishes, or anything they try to do. As a teen's understanding about death evolves, questions may naturally come up about mortality and vulnerability. Teens also tend to search more for meaning in the death of someone close to them. A teen who asks why someone had to die probably isn't looking for literal answers, but starting to explore the idea of the meaning of life. Even to this very day, I still find myself answering questions and/or explaining things to my kids about my mother and grandmother's situations before they passed away. The desire for even more knowledge and understanding is presenting itself within my kids and I pray that God continue to bless me with the insight and answers to be able to share it with them. I won't know all of the answers to their questions but, for the most part, I've sufficiently tackled them all.

Recently, my daughter explained that she dreamed about my mother and saw her with wings on her back as she entered my kids' bedroom. The ironic thing about this is, I dreamed about my mother on this same exact night, but never mentioned anything to my kids until my daughter revealed her dream to me and my sons one morning. In my daughter's dream, she said my mother hugged all of us closely with a smile on her face.

After the prolonged, comforting hug, my daughter said that my mother turned back around and exited the bedroom, revealing the wings she had on her back. In my dream, I saw my mother in the healthy state that she was in before she was diagnosed with ovarian cancer two years ago. Just like my daughter explained, I also saw a smile on my mother's face, as she sat at her dining room table talking with me and my other family members like she used to do. Man, I tell you, this is one of those dreams that a person will wake up from wishing it was still a reality. However, when I thought about it, again, I realized that it probably is a reality even though I just can't visibly see it while I'm awake. Remember, I explained earlier how the spirits of a deceased loved one can still communicate with us within our dreams. My mother came to my daughter in her dream to show her that she's ok. Not only is she ok, she also received her wings and is watching over us just like I explained to my kids several times before.

My mother also validated this confirmation with me as well because; she knows my heart still grieves today, just as much as it did when I witnessed her take her final breath. To anyone who's reading this, please don't allow negative people who don't believe or understand anything about the spiritual world stir you in the wrong direction with false information. When people don't believe in something, they'll try to discourage your belief too.

Chapter Four   **The Toll That Death Has On Kids**

Although most of us will find ways to accept and live with the loss of a loved one, don't think for a second that a person will ever truly get over this loss. If you've ever been told that you would, I'm here now to tell you differently from experience. The pain is too extreme for a person to ever fully get over it. Most of us just learn how to deal with it and try to move on to the best of our ability. With time, a person has the ability to move on much better, but the void of losing someone close to you will always be there, no matter what. Knowing that, that person is still with you in spirit, although you'd quite obviously prefer to still have them in the physical, seems to help me out. One thing I've also learned and the same applies to kids as well is, don't remain stuck on one particular emotion for too long. In my case, my first reaction and emotion that urgently revealed its face openly after I saw my mother pass away was anger. I was extremely angry for multiple reasons: (feeling as though I was let down by God and made a fool of in front of everyone who just knew how things would end, knowing my life had to continue on now without my mother and grandmother, and the list can go on and on).

Then dealing with society and how this world operates most times doesn't make things any better. In a child's case, it's also extremely important to monitor any prolonged behavior patterns that doesn't demonstrate their normal characteristics and personalities.

A child's best teacher is their parent so, in order for me to teach them how to handle grief and do their best to move on in life, I had to demonstrate just that, finding a way in the process to set my anger aside. To help you understand how different age groups of children react to death and how you can assist them more effectively, I'll share this information with you as well.

Children younger than age 3:

Children of this age have little or no understanding of death. If the deceased is a parent or other close person in their life, they may react to the separation and any change of routine or environment. They are likely to search, cry and overall be upset and clingy. They may also change their sleep or eating habits.

For children this age it is important for parents to try to maintain normality as much as possible, and minimize any impact on the child. Provide extra attention and affection when needed, and be patient and understanding with any 'acting out' behavior.

Chapter Four   **The Toll That Death Has On Kids**

Children aged 3-5:

Children of this age have some understanding of death, but it is likely to them to mean a change in living circumstances. They will struggle to realize the finality of death, and may believe it is reversible. They may also ask many questions and try to personalize the experience, even believing it was caused by them. Children of this age may feel angry, sad and worried and express their emotions through tantrums, clinging, regression to behaviors such as bed-wetting, nightmares, etc. They may feel scared that other people close to them will die too, or act as though the deceased is still alive.

For children this age, parents need to be patient with questions and answer them as openly as possible. Try to avoid confusing descriptions such as 'gone to sleep'. Though this may be easier to say, it is likely to confuse a small child. Emphasize the fact that the deceased person is not in pain or suffering. Modeling appropriate grief can also be important to show them it's ok to be upset and sad.

Children aged 6-9:

Children of this age are able to comprehend simple details about how a person died, such as from disease or in an accident.

They are likely to concentrate on concrete details such as that a dead person is buried in the ground, or is taken away by a special car. However their emotions can often not match their level of cognitive understanding. They may also develop beliefs that their thoughts can cause bad things to happen. Children of this age may feel denial, anger, self-blame or irritability. Their moods may fluctuate and they may become withdrawn and struggle to concentrate.

Children of this age need to be reassured they are not to blame. It may be helpful to give them mechanisms to express their grief, perhaps through painting, drawing, music, letters to the deceased, or making memory boxes. Concrete actions like these may help them come to terms with the death and the sense of loss they feel. They may also need extra support with schooling and home chores.

Children aged 9-12:
Children of this age are likely to understand the finality of death, and that it will happen to everyone at some time. They may feel different, or as though they need to put on a brave face. They may also feel protective of others. They may become aggressive or resentful, and experience disturbed sleep, isolation and suppressed emotions.

Chapter Four   **The Toll That Death Has On Kids**

They may also become preoccupied with their physical health or school performance. Children of this age may need a lot of emotional support from parents and peers. They may even need professional counseling. As parents, you may need support for yourself and guidance from others about the best ways to help your child. So far for me, I've been handling this on my own.

Teens and adolescents:

Teenagers understand the full implications of death. As such, they may feel resentful and concerned about the future. They are likely to question their own mortality and may be scared of exposing their emotions. They may experience anger, anxiety, resentment, self-involvement, fear of death, avoidance of feelings, guilt and distance. They may engage in risky behaviors and 'act out', or become apathetic and withdrawn.

Children of this age may need time and patience to work through their feelings. They may come into conflict with you or others, so it is important to give them space and support them however you can. They may seek support from peers or others close to them, which should be encouraged. They may also need professional counseling.

Chapter Four   The Toll That Death Has On Kids

Throughout all of these stages, as I stated before, it's extremely important to monitor a child's progress through time and seek guidance from a mental health professional if you have any concerns. They may be able to offer you advice or point you towards appropriate support for you or your child. It's also important to recognize your own feelings, and seek relevant support for yourself so you can be there for your child/children. The death of a loved one is heart-wrenching, strenuous, overly depressing and any other synonymous term that goes hand-in-hand with describing pain. If you're blessed enough to still have close family members within your grasp, hold onto them as tightly as you possibly can, put all differences aside and look out for one another to the best of your ability. Time is very limited for us as human beings on this earth and, now is the time to wake up and appreciate whatever it is you may have, no matter how great or how small it may be because, the next second isn't promised to any of us. In the next chapter, I'm going to take things a step further by explaining what the Spiritual Warfare is all about. I'll also provide information that enables you to understand how God equipped us with the proper armor that's required in order for us to become victorious in this Spiritual Warfare.

Spiritual Warfare

Sometimes, when a person life is coming to an end and they're transitioning over to the spiritual world, you might hear them fearfully screaming out or, nervously flinching as if they're tremendously terrified by the images they're seeing. In this case, they may be seeing spiritual demons which are sent to them by Satan himself as an attempt to steal their spirit/soul. I can't express enough the importance of praying to God, especially during these end-of-life stages, to prevent Satan from successfully accomplishing his task. It's bad enough that Satan wants our souls while we're alive, tempting us in various formations that can lead to our very own self-inflicting torture as a result if we follow through on his wicked invites.

Have you ever found yourself going to sleep at night, only to wake up the next morning feeling completely drained as if you hadn't been to sleep in the first place? Often times this is the result of a spiritual warfare occurring while you're supposed to be getting rest from sleeping. Spiritual Warfare is basically the struggle to have life in this material world reflect as much as possible, God's governance. Thing very thing that causes it to result in a war is the forces that work vigorously to thwart what God is doing.

Throughout it all, God is always in control, but there is an enemy that's in full-scale revolt, and has powerful influences all around. It's a whole lot that's going on in the Spiritual World right now but we just can't see it as its happening. As with the invisible, unseen God, the forces that are behind the revolt are unseen as well. However, these forces lust after power in the world of visible, material beings. Just because we can't see the battle taking place doesn't mean it's not going on. The problem with some people in this world is, if they can't see it, they won't believe or accept it. They'll continue to live in denial and blinded just like Satan prefers for them to be.

One key factor to almost remember is, the Devil has already lost the battle, he's just trying to take as many souls and spirits with him as he can possibly take, as an attempt to hurt God. Every time Satan succeeds in doing so, God hurts - - the same pain that a parent feels over losing a child. Satan can be described in different forms; a leech ranks at the top of the list as one of his descriptions. Satan is lacking so much in life that, the only life he honestly have left is what he sucks out of us humans. Another way to describe the Devil is by using the term 'sham', a face without a person behind it, all apparitions but no substance. Satan can always overpower us with temptations, but he can never fully be because he's limited; powerful but limited.

Satan's main purpose is to continuously plot evil, working against God's plan for redemption, eternal life and restoration. The Devil is a furious spirit, mainly because he was casted down from Heaven along with other Dark Angels. Most of us don't realize it because of the daily struggles we're overwhelmed with here on earth but, God has equipped us with the Heavenly armor needed to battle against the enemy. From my studies, I've learned that there is a six piece Heavenly Armor a true Christian can utilize during Spiritual Warfare that'll result in the defeat of the enemy every time. The first of these six is to always '*Hold Your Ground*' having tightened the belt of truth around your loins.

Truth is a Godly value, our spiritual belt of protection around our loins - - the core of our body. The Bible teaches that we must worship God in spirit and in truth. (John 4:24). God loves the truth because he has made Jesus the way, the truth, and the life. When we walk, speak and live in truth, we know that we are spiritually protected by God because it's in his nature. God despises lies. That's what the Devil specializes in, Deception and Lies. In contrast, the Bible says that Satan hates the truth because there is no truth in him. When he lies it is consistent with his character, because he is a liar and the father of all lies.

Next, '*Lift Up Over All The Covering Shield Of Saving Faith.*'
What I mean by this is faith can be used as our shield against
the enemy. Every dart the enemy attempts to annihilate us
with, God will intercept, causing it to crumble to the ground
with no effect on us whatsoever. After doing those two things,
'*Taking the Helmet of Salvation*' is our next piece of armor.
Repent; accept Jesus Christ as your personal Lord and Savior.
Believe that God raised him from the dead for the forgiveness
of our sins, enabling us to have eternal life with Christ
someday. Go throughout your day knowing without a doubt
that you have the protection of God over you.

When you've mastered these things, move on to '*Putting on
the Breastplate of Integrity and of Moral Rectitude.*' By doing
this it symbolizes that your intentions are good and Godly,
meaning no harm against another. This is a trait that God loves
in his people, his Holy Nation. It is a reflection of God and his
goodness and we must wear it as a spiritual weapon on honor
on our chest. We're made in God's image, it's our identity and
it's who we are.

Then, when you're ready to put on the next piece of armor,
*Shod Your Feet [in Preparation to Face the Enemy Firm-
Footed, Ready to Produce the Good News]*. Throughout the
day we want to find a way to hold the peace of God in our
spirit and in our heart.

Lastly, unleash our offensive weapon which is known as the *'Sword of Spirit.'* If you can imagine how a metal sword can destructively pierce through flesh and bone, this is exactly how God's word pierces and guts out the enemy. The Word of God is our empowerment, super-natural favor for us that keeps the enemy at bay. Always be aware that Spiritual warfare comes in two ways: offensive and defensive. Offensive warfare is tearing down the strongholds the enemy has formed in your mind through deception and accusations, and defensive warfare is guarding yourself against the tactics or schemes of the Devil. There are three things that we can expect from the devil. The Bible tells us that we struggle not against flesh and blood, but against demonic forces. [Ephesians 6:12], "For we wrestle not against flesh and blood, but against principalities, against powers, against the rulers of the darkness of this world, against spiritual wickedness in high places."

Having said this, I'll share with you what the three primary things we struggle against consist of. Right off the top, **Deception** is the first element I'll elaborate on. Deception quite obviously means to make another person believe a lie or something that is not true. When the enemy sends deception your way, it is an attempt to deceive you into believing something that is not true, so you will fall into error.

Strongholds are built through deception. A stronghold is formed when deception takes hold in a person's mind. A stronghold is an incorrect thinking pattern that stems from believing something that is not true. From the very beginning, Satan deceived Eve into believing that God's Word was not true. In Genesis 3:4, the Devil told her that she will not surely die as God said she would in Genesis 2:17.

Temptation often follows deception. First the enemy tells us, "You won't surely die!", and then he makes the fruit on the forbidden tree look good to us. Since Eve accepted Satan's deception (his lie), now the tree that she was not supposed to touch looked good to her. She was tempted (enticed) to sin, because she allowed herself to first be deceived. Temptation is when we are enticed or encouraged to sin in one way or another.

In Matthew 4, Jesus was led out in the desert to be tempted by the Devil. The Devil tried to convince Jesus that it would be harmless to jump off a building. Often people will be so drawn to sex with their boyfriend/girlfriend when the enemy tries to convince them that it is all harmless and fun, when it's not harmless at all, but an open door to the Devil. Jesus saw through Satan's deception, and resisted the temptation by speaking God's Word. King David said in Psalms 119:11, "Thy word have I hid in mine heart, that I might not sin against thee."

When the enemy tempts you, he's showing you the worm... but behind that worm is a hook. The Word of God helps you see the hook behind the worm.

Accusations ranks in at number three on the list. The Devil is known as the accuser of the brethren (Rev 12:10). He is known to take a believer who has done an embarrassing or gross sin in their past, and continue to rub it in their faces and beat them down with guilt and condemnation over their past.

A stronghold is deception that's taken hold in a person's mind. It's an incorrect thinking pattern based on a believed lie. People can get incorrect perceptions of God by listening to Satan as he tells them how God doesn't love them, etc. People can feel like dirty old sinners when they believe Satan's accusations as he continually reminds them of their past (which has been washed away!). Strongholds are based on lies from the devil. They can come in the form of deception or accusations. Accusations always lead to guilt and the feeling of unworthiness, which weighs you down and tears you apart spiritually.

Since strongholds are built upon lies that we have been fed, the way we tear down strongholds is by feeding on the truth (in God's Word), which is the opposite of what the enemy has been feeding us. If the enemy has been feeding us a lie, we need to stop eating the lie and start feeding ourselves the truth.

The weapon we use to tear down strongholds is found in Ephesians 6:17, "...the sword of the Spirit that I mentioned a minute ago. A sword is an offensive weapon and is meant to tear down and kill the enemy's troops. Strongholds are the Devil's assets in war, and he uses them against us. Take up the sword of the Spirit (God's Word) today, and start slaughtering the enemy's assets that he's been using against you!

In the next and final chapter, I'm going to highlight a few things we've already discussed, show you a chart which breaks down the exact location of our soul and spirit, comparison of the human body to the subtle body (after death) and a few other pieces of information I'd like to share with you before reaching the conclusion of this book.

Summary of What Happens After Death

Spiritual research shows that a human being is comprised of the following four basic bodies (physical, mental, causal or intellectual and subtle ego). When a person dies the physical body ceases to exist. However, the rest of his/her existence continues. The existence of a person minus the physical body is known as the subtle body and it comprises the mental, causal (intellect) bodies. This subtle body then goes to one of the 13 subtle planes of existence other than the earthly realm.

Be mindful that there are 14 planes of existence in the Universe. Seven of these planes are positive planes and the other seven are negative planes of existence. The seven negative planes of existence are commonly known as Hell. There are also numerous amounts of sub-planes within these main planes of existence as well. First, take a look at the diagram chart I've provided on the next page. Afterwards, I'll elaborate on what these 14 planes (positive and negative mainly consist of).

Seven positive planes of existence: The planes of existence occupied mostly by living persons and subtle bodies doing righteous deeds and engaged in spiritual practice according to the positive path of spiritual practice are known as the seven positive planes of existence or *sapta-loka*. By positive path, I mean the orientation of spiritual practice is towards God-realization, which is the ultimate in spiritual growth.

The Earth plane is the only physical plane of existence in the Universe and is also the first plane of existence in the hierarchy of the positive planes of existence in the Universe.

Seven Negative planes of existence: These are planes of existence occupied mostly by subtle bodies that have done unrighteous deeds and are engaged in spiritual practice according to the negative path. By negative path, I mean the orientation of spiritual practice is towards attaining spiritual power, e.g. supernatural powers. This spiritual power is primarily used to enhance one's control over others or for negative purposes. Thus all subtle bodies that go to any one of the planes of existence of Hell, by virtue of their evil intentions become ghosts. Sub planes of existence of Hell (*Narak*): Every plane of existence of Hell (Paataal) has a sub-plane known as *Narak*. For example, the first plane of existence of Hell will have within it a sub-plane that is known as the first *Narak*. *Narak* is reserved for the worst ghosts (demons, devils, negative energies, etc.) in Hell.

The ghosts, demons, devils, negative energy, etc. that occupy the first *Narak* face more severe punishment and for a longer duration than those occupying the first plane of existence of Hell. Each positive and negative plane of existence beyond the Earth (physical) plane of existence becomes more and more subtle. Subtle meaning, that which is beyond the comprehension of the five senses, mind and intellect. *Satyaloka* is the subtlest, i.e. the most difficult to perceive or comprehend unless the highest sixth sense (ESP) level is attained.

Due to lack of spiritual practice, most people in the current era go to either the Nether world or one of the planes of existence of Hell. We generally go to the Nether world after death when the proportion of demerits (incurred due to wrong doings on Earth) is approximately 30%. Demerits typically include malice towards others and a lot of desires. The likelihood of being attacked in the Nether world by higher-level ghosts from the lower plane of existence of Hell is almost certain.

Earth is the only plane of existence where there is an amalgamation of people with varying spiritual levels. However, after death we go to the precise plane of existence corresponding to our spiritual level.

The minimum spiritual level required to attain Heaven after death is 60%.

Chapter Six   Summary of What Happens After Death

Basically from the Spiritual science perspective, meritorious acts to attain Heaven or the higher positive planes of existence are those acts done with the objective of God-realization. The following three criteria can be applied.

*Acts done without doer ship, i.e. with the outlook that God Himself is getting it done from me and hence I cannot lay claim to any credit.

*Done without expectation of acclaim or appreciation.

*Done without expectation of results.

More than the acts per se, it is the attitude or outlook behind the acts that counts more.

To attain a higher plane of existence beyond Heaven one needs to be at a spiritual level higher than 80%. This can only be achieved by consistent spiritual practice according to the six basic laws of spiritual practice along with a major reduction in ego.

By predominant body, I mean the body that is most active, i.e., mental, intellect or the subtle ego. For example, in the Nether plane of existence (*Bhuvalok*), the subtle bodies still have a lot of desires and attachments. As a result, quite often they become ghosts trying to fulfill some desire of theirs.

Chapter Six   Summary of What Happens After Death

This leaves them open to higher-level ghosts from the lower rungs of Hell to take advantage of their cravings to affect people on Earth.

In the Nether plane of existence we experience some happiness. However, the unhappiness is amplified as compared to the unhappiness experienced on Earth.

In Heaven plane of existence, subtle bodies experience an over abundance of happiness. This happiness is much beyond the happiness experienced on Earth in quantity, quality and duration. As we go up the positive planes of existence, there is an increase in the quality of happiness and no unhappiness.

Sattvik happiness means happiness derived from helping others without any expectations or strings attached. When ego is involved in the act, it becomes *raajasik*.

Serenity is a higher experience than Bliss. From the planes of existence below *Mahālok*, people need to be reincarnated on the Earth plane to settle their destiny and complete their give-and-take accounts.

If one attains *Mahālok* and *Janalok* after death, that means they are above the spiritual level of 80%. These souls do not need to be reincarnated as all their remaining destiny (accumulated account) can be worked out from these planes itself.

However these evolved subtle bodies may choose to be born of their own will. They do so primarily to act as spiritual guides for humanity.

In some circumstances people who pass away at the spiritual level of even 60% can attain *Mahālok*. Here the person's potential for further spiritual growth is considered. Through spiritual research we have found that that there are 5 factors that influence this potential for further spiritual growth.

Having a high amount of spiritual emotion

Having a low ego,

Having an intense desire for spiritual growth

Doing regular spiritual practice of increasingly higher levels,

Affected or not affected by negative energies.

Being affected by negative energies can severely obstruct the ability for spiritual growth. Hence even if a person is at the 65% spiritual level but is severely affected by negative energies, his ability to attain the higher spiritual planes of existence such as *Mahālok*, is restricted.

Chapter Six   Summary of What Happens After Death

If one attains *Tapalok* or *Satyalok* after death, then one does not take birth on the Earth plane of existence but continues to do spiritual practice from that plane of existence until one merges completely with God. The Earth plane of existence is very important. It is the only plane of existence where we can make rapid spiritual growth and settle our give-and-take account in the shortest period of time. The main reason for this is that with the help of the physical body, we can do many things to enhance our spiritual growth and spiritual level and reduce the basic subtle *tama* component.

Other than Earth, spiritual growth is mostly likely to occur only in the regions beyond Heaven such as *Mahaaloka* etc. This is because in Heaven, the subtle bodies run the risk of getting caught up in the unending pleasures it offers. In the Nether and Hell planes of existence, the punishment is so severe and also the distress from the other higher-level ghosts is such that it becomes very difficult to rise above the suffering to undertake any spiritual practice of value. As one goes to lower planes of existence in Hell, as the subtle basic sattva component progressively reduces the environment becomes less conducive to the experience of happiness. Within the planes of existence of Hell, there are some ghosts who do certain types of spiritual practice to gain spiritual power. The highest in the hierarchy of ghosts are sorcerers from the seventh plane of existence of Hell.

Chapter Six   Summary of What Happens After Death

They have immense spiritual power almost equivalent to a Saint at the 90% spiritual level. They control all the other types of ghosts with lesser spiritual power.

As one goes deeper into the various planes of existence of Hell, i.e. from 1st to 7th, the extent of happiness experienced by the subtle bodies therein goes on decreasing and the extent of unhappiness goes on multiplying. The minimal experience of happiness is also due to being engrossed in memories of past positive events, pleasant memories of wealth in a past life, etc. The experience of unhappiness is due to memories of physical pain and insulting events, memories of unfulfilled desires, e.g. regarding education, house, career, expectation of happiness from children in past life.

The extent of punishment/pain to be endured in the various planes of existence of Hell (*Paataal*) and their associated *Narak* goes on increasing with the subsequent plane of existence of Hell. Also, the period of punishment to be endured in each *Narak* is in excess compared to the corresponding plane of existence of Hell. If we consider the punishment in first plane of existence of Hell as 100%, then the punishment in the corresponding first *Narak* region is 50% more, i.e. 150%.

Chapter Six   **Summary of What Happens After Death**

One is assigned that plane of existence which matches one's basic nature in terms of *sattva, raja and tama.* This is also a function of one's spiritual level. Hence, subtle bodies from lower positive planes of existence cannot go to higher positive planes of existence and those from first or second negative planes of existence cannot go to the deeper planes of existence Hell. This is similar to how people living in the planes find breathing difficult at higher altitudes, but people staying at higher altitudes manage fine.

At the time of death, as the physical body becomes inactive the vital energy used for the functioning of the physical body is liberated into the Universe. This vital energy at the time of death propels the subtle body away from the Earth region. Just as the weight of a projectile decides how far a rocket will propel it, similarly the weight of the subtle body decides which plane of existence it goes to in the subtle planes of existence in life after death.

The 'weight' of the subtle body is primarily a function of the amount of the subtle basic *tama* component in our being. Each one of us is made up of three subtle basic components or *gunas*. These components are spiritual in nature and cannot be seen but they define our personalities.

They are:

Sattva: Purity and knowledge

Raja: Action and passion

Tama: Ignorance and inertia in an average person in the current era, the basic subtle *tama* component is as high as 50%.

The more we are filled with the *raja* and *tama* components the more we display the following characteristics which add to our 'weight' and impact which plane of existence we go to in our life after death:

More attachment to worldly things and selfishness

More unfulfilled desires

Feelings of revenge

Higher amount of demerits or wrong-doings

Higher amount of personality defects such as anger, greed, fear, etc.

A higher amount of ego: By ego we mean how much a person identifies himself with his body, mind and intellect as opposed to the soul within, resulting in lower spiritual level.

Chapter Six   **Summary of What Happens After Death**

A permanent reduction in the proportion of the subtle basic *tama* component and the related characteristics mentioned above come about only with sustained spiritual practice according to the six basic laws of spiritual practice. Psychological improvements with self-help books or trying to be nice are at best superficial and temporary. The mental state at the point of death, apart from what has been mentioned above, is very important. Our mental state is generally relative to the proportion of the subtle basic components in our being.

If a person is actually doing his spiritual practice such as chanting the name of God at the time of death then the influence of desires, attachments, ghosts, etc. are minimal possible for that person compared to his state when not chanting. This makes his subtle body lighter. Hence, if he/she passes away while chanting, he attains better plane of existence among the sub-planes than what he would have attained were he/she to pass away without chanting.

At the time of death, if a person is chanting the Name of God and is also in a state of surrender to God's will, then he/she attains an even better plane of existence in his life after death and his sojourn is undertaken with lightening speed. This is because the person being in a state of surrender on Earth plane of existence itself has very less chance of increasing his/her ego in their life after death.

Chapter Six   **Summary of What Happens After Death**

There are two types of death with regards to its timing.

Destined final death: This is the time of death that no one can escape.

Possible death: This is where a person can possibly die. Each person may undergo a possible death wherein one comes close to death but may be saved due to his or her merits.

In cases where a person is going through insurmountable crisis in his life or has severe personality disorders, he may think of taking his own life in a depressed state. Demonic forces also fuel the depression of a suicidal person and sometimes are instrumental in pushing a person over the edge into committing suicide. However, suicide remains a willful act that happens when a person is going through a possible death phase as per their destiny.

Life on the Earth plane of existence is precious and is given to us primarily for spiritual growth. When we kill others we create a *kārmic* give and take account with them. However by committing suicide, we squander away the opportunity for spiritual growth and hence incur the heaviest sin.

Chapter Six   Summary of What Happens After Death

The consequences are that a person committing suicide goes to the *Narak* part of the 7th plane of existence of Hell for a period of 60,000 Earth years, in his/her life after death. It is a place that is without any light; something like solitary confinement in a prison. As there is nobody in that *Narak* region who can give advice about spiritual practice, the subtle body remains in the darkness of spiritual ignorance. The above facts about the various planes of existence give us a fair idea of the possible consequences in our life after death of how we live our lives. Only with spiritual practice or with extreme meritorious deeds can one go to the higher planes of existence and thereby avoid unhappiness and punishment and enjoy higher levels of happiness. There are also better chances of a reincarnation on Earth plane of existence in circumstances conducive to spiritual practice. This is so that one moves further up in the subtle planes of existence in the Universe. As we go further into the current Era of Strife (*Kaliyuga*), there is lesser likelihood of people going to the higher planes of existence.

Once we go to the lower planes of existence such as the Nether plane of existence or other planes of existence of Hell, we stay there and experience severe unhappiness for centuries until we completely pay for our demerits (sins) by suffering the intense punishments meted there and get a chance to be reincarnated on Earth.

Chapter Six   Summary of What Happens After Death

To do consistent spiritual practice on the Earth plane of existence according to the 6 basic laws of spiritual practice is like swimming against the tide in the current era. However, it is also a guaranteed way of advancing to higher planes of existence in our life after death. In closing, I hope my personal experiences that I've shared openly in this book, combined with the educational information I've also provided, will help anyone who may be reading this. Even when I'm going through the toughest times in my personal life, I still try to find ways to bring some type of positive results out of it. It's nothing positive about losing a loved one, like I've explained in my case with my mother and grandmother, back to back. However, several people in this world are going through this same experience in their lives or, have experienced it in the past, which will enable them to identify easily with the text I've provided. Through my pain, I'm reaching out to anyone who may be reading this, making you fully aware that you're not alone. Always remember that a Spiritual World does exist and, although your loved ones are not with you physically, they'll always be with you in spirit until you see them again. Keep them near and dear to your heart and, whenever you're alone, talk to them, they're listening. God bless you all!

Acknowledgments

As always, it's extremely important to me that I thank our Heavenly Father first and foremost, for giving me the gift of being a writer so I can have some type of platform that enables me to reach out and connect with anyone who purchases my material. This book is my sixth release and, it's dedicated to the memory of my mother and grandmother (Lisa and Lucille Lynch). May you both Rest In Peace. To my kids, Jerome Jr., Ja'ron and Jasmine, I love you all from the bottom of my heart. To my aunt, Marcella, words can't express how much I appreciate you for being the only adult family member that was willing to put on your armor and stand side-by-side with me, giving it your all to help take care of my mother when no one else would step up to do so. I'm extremely appreciative of you beyond measures. To my readers and supporters who've spent their hard earned money to support me, I'm highly appreciative of you as well and, I pray that you continue to follow me and the projects I release in the near future. Until next time, God bless you all.

Jerome Staten

Contact Info:

www.facebook.com/jeromestaten

jerome_staten@yahoo.com